GOOD TIME CHARLIE
One Family's Journey from Addiction to Salvation

Robbie Leffel

Copyright © 2022 by Robbie Leffel

All Scripture quotations are taken from: The Holy Bible, English Standard Version, ESV® Text Edition: 2016. Copyright © 2001 by Crossway, a publishing ministry of Good News Publishers. The ESV® text has been reproduced in cooperation with and by permission of Good News Publishers. All rights reserved worldwide.

All rights reserved. No part of this book may be reproduced or transmitted in any form or by any means, electronic or mechanical, including photocopying, recording or by any information storage and retrieval system, without permission in writing from the Publisher.

First published in the United States of America in 2022
by Robbie Leffel

Library of Congress Cataloging-in-Publication Data
Robbie Leffel
p. cm.

Cover photo by Robbie Leffel

ISBN 978-0-578-35529-0

DEDICATION

I dedicate this book to my family. First to my mom, Delores, and my sister, Lorrie Ann. You both walked much of this journey with me through the highs and the lows. Some things we would like to forget and some things we will cherish forever. God used every step to help us grow closer to him. I love you both more than you know.

I can't leave out my wife and love of my life, Darenda. If it wasn't for you, I am not sure anyone would be hearing me talk about Jesus today. You were the spiritual leader of our home for many years. I am so thankful for your tenacity to make sure our two beautiful daughters, Danielle Nicole and Deidra Danay, got involved in church and were introduced to Jesus.

Nanny Leffel, I know you're in heaven now, but I can't leave you out. You were our rock. I don't know how you held it together all those years with the challenges of our family, but you persevered.

Thank you all for loving me and never giving up.

TABLE OF CONTENTS

Introduction 7
Chapter 1 Seizures, Swamp Coolers, and Hard Work 9
Chapter 2 The Accident 13
Chapter 3 The Good Life 17
Chapter 4 Fresh Starts and Hidden Bottles 21
Chapter 5 Alcohol Takes Control 25
Chapter 6 Good Time Charlie 29
Chapter 7 Jesus Saves 33
Chapter 8 Downhill Spiral 35
Chapter 9 Shock Treatment and Near Misses 39
Chapter 10 Football and Jesus 43
Chapter 11 Drinking Bars and Prison Bars 47
Chapter 12 Surprise! 51
Chapter 13 The Real World 55
Chapter 14 On the Move Chasing a Career 59
Chapter 15 The Reload Revival 65
Chapter 16 Jesus Prepares Me 69
Chapter 17 The Call for Help 73
Chapter 18 The Struggle for True Forgiveness 77
Chapter 19 Obstacles 81
Chapter 20 The Ride 85
Chapter 21 A Changed Heart 89
Chapter 22 Forgiveness 95
About the Author 99

INTRODUCTION

Ever since the day my father, Charles Edwin Leffel—a.k.a. Good Time Charlie—passed away, I've had this feeling I needed to write a book about him and our journey.

Dad was a very simple man who lived a very challenging life. Because of circumstances in his life, he went down a path of tremendous heartache and loss, not only for him, but also his entire family. He had something missing in his life, and he tried to fill it with booze, his wife, kids, and work.

But nothing he was chasing could heal the deep wounds he carried. As time went on, the more frequently he turned to the bottle.

I think this story will speak to people who have experienced or are currently going through some of the challenges our family faced. I hope this book will encourage and open hearts to forgiveness.

In this book, I share the story of my father and the tragic loss of his friend's life in a horrible accident—and the impact this event had on Dad and his family for the rest of his life.

Most of this story is shared through my eyes beginning as a child until my dad's passing.

My father's roller-coaster tale has taught me several key lessons, all centered on the everlasting hope we have in our savior, Jesus Christ: Jesus offers the loving forgiveness we all need, which can only be found in Him; Jesus changed my life, and He used me to reach my father; and we should never give up hope.

God is bigger than any problem, any addiction, and any pain.

—*Robbie Leffel*
October 7, 2021

CHAPTER 1
Seizures, Swamp Coolers, and Hard Work

My dad, "Good Time Charlie," was born Charles Edwin Leffel in a house out in the country near Cuthand, Texas, on March 6, 1942. He was the only child of Charles "Red" Melvin Leffel and Cora Ada Byrd Leffel, who moved from east Texas to the Texas Panhandle in the early 1950s. They worked in and around the Panhandle and eventually settled in Hereford, Texas, southwest of Amarillo.

My grandparents were simple, hardworking people living on little to nothing. My grandfather, whom I called Pa Leffel, worked for the City of Hereford on a trash truck loading 55-gallon trash barrels every day of the workweek. He also collected aluminum, copper, Coke bottles—anything he could do to make an extra dollar. My grandmother, Nanny Leffel, worked numerous jobs over the years, from sorting potatoes in the "tater sheds," ironing and folding clothes at laundromats, and finally as a cook at La Plata Junior High School. She made rolls from scratch every single day.

Diligent and trustworthy, you could always count on both of them. They never missed a day of work. They were committed, and besides, they needed the work. Nanny told me the most money they ever made in one year together was less than $20,000—for the entire year. They didn't spend much, mainly purchasing groceries, giving to the church, and saving.

I don't know much about my dad's upbringing, but my grandmother told me my grandfather was pretty hard on my dad, and he disciplined harshly. He'd whip my dad with a belt, at times violently. Disciplining your child with a belt wasn't unusual during those times, but my grandfather was excessive in his punishment. Needless to say, they didn't have the best relationship.

My dad, Charles Edwin Leffel, was the only child of Charles "Red" Melvin Leffel and Cora Ada Byrd Leffel.

I have pictures from those old days, and everyone looks happy, but pictures don't always tell the real story. As long as I can remember, there was tension between my dad and his dad. Pa Leffel had epilepsy, which caused seizures. Nobody really understood epilepsy back then, and people were quick to judge when he had a seizure. They would say, "He's crazy," or "He's having fits." Many of his seizures occurred in public, and as you can imagine, people looked at him like he was a monster. They just didn't understand what was happening.

The epilepsy was hard on the whole family. My grandmother worried about him all the time, especially fearful he'd have a seizure and either hurt himself or someone else. People made fun behind my grandfather's

My dad and his parents lived in an 800-square-foot house in Hereford, Texas, with four rooms and a bathroom.

back, and the other kids teased my father about his crazy dad and his crazy spells. I know that had to be embarrassing for my dad, and the fact that they didn't get along only made things worse. He was mortified by his dad's condition.

My dad and his parents lived in an 800-square-foot house, 216 Whiteface, across the street from Shirley Elementary and Hereford High School. The house was not much more than a roof and some walls. White and made of sod, it had a couple of windows in the front, a couple in the back, and a front and back door. It had four rooms and a bathroom, and the way the house was built inside, you could walk through every room of the house in less than ten seconds, so saying it was small was accurate. The house originally had dirt floors, and at first they didn't even have a toilet—they used an outhouse. I was told the city forced my grandfather in the late 1950s to add indoor plumbing to replace the outhouse, so the house was even smaller before the city came along.

Pa Leffel had a reputation for watching his money very closely. Rumor was that he had a Buffalo head nickel, and twice a day he'd go down to the cellar and wipe its rear. I have no idea if that was true, but it makes me laugh to picture it.

I spent a lot of time at this house, and though it wasn't much, I loved being there. I remember those long, hot summer nights with the doors open and the swamp cooler running, hearing the train pass through town.

For me, it was a place of consistency. I knew what to expect, and I could always count on my grandparents. They were always available when we needed them.

CHAPTER 2
The Accident

My dad struggled in school. Nanny said academics were tough for him from the very beginning. He never made good grades and, between his dad's seizures and their lack of money, probably felt looked down on by others.

As you can imagine, when school is such a struggle you don't put in your greatest effort. You find other things to occupy your time. So along came my mom, Delores Price.

Mom was around 14 years old when she and Dad met and fell in love, and he was about 15. As I look back, man—they were so different. In fact, I often wondered how they ever got together. My dad was a bit of a bad boy, skipping school, drinking, and smoking cigarettes. Mom was just the opposite. She was active in school, made very good grades, and had lots of friends, so maybe it's true that opposites attract. I think life was fairly normal for my dad's blue-collar family working and trying to make a living. One thing for sure is my dad was crazy about my mom from the day he met her, and though they didn't stay together because of many challenges and hurdles, he never stopped loving her.

Life for everyone changed on Monday, October 28, 1957, when my dad was 15. That day after school, my dad and a couple of his school buddies decided to go back to his house to see a brand-new .410 shotgun my grandfather had bought. This type of gun was not common, so they were all excited to take a look.

My dad pulled the shotgun out of the closet and began to show the boys. Everyone was excited to see the new gun, as it was a bolt-action gun, which was different from most of the guns at that time.

He tried to open the chamber, but a shell was stuck, and he rattled the lever to try to get the shell out.

That's when the gun went off.

His good friend Billy Lee Madden, just 12 years old but one of my dad's closest friends, was standing right beside him. When the gun went off, the shot struck Billy at point-blank range.

Billy fell in that hallway and never got up. He died right beside my dad. It was Dad's worst nightmare.

From that day forward, life for everyone was never the same. Nanny told me someone got in touch with her at the laundromat to tell her there had been an accident at her house. As you can imagine, she was terrified. She hurried as fast as she could to get home to find out exactly what happened.

By the time she got home, the police and ambulance were there, and she found out that young man had lost his life.

"What did you do?" I asked her years later.

Nanny sighed and bowed her head. "I cried—and then I cleaned up the blood in the hallway."

I can't even imagine how they all must have felt. The police immediately ruled it an accident, as all the boys told them what had happened. I never spoke to my dad about the specifics, and he never volunteered anything else, only how he felt so much guilt it was overwhelming. He just didn't know how to handle it.

Devastated and heartbroken, Dad immediately dropped out of school and moved in with Nanny's oldest brother, my dad's Uncle Elbert "Red" Byrd, who was the deputy sheriff 95 miles north in Dalhart, Texas. Dad had to get away from Hereford. The shame and guilt were almost unbearable. I'm not sure how long he stayed in Dalhart, but I can only imagine those long, lonely hours reliving that fateful day over and over in his head.

My grandmother was heartbroken about the accident, as well as about my dad leaving and what he was going through emotionally. For his part, Pa Leffel felt embarrassed and horribly guilty. The whole community was talking about our family. The stares and whispers felt like daggers when he walked by. In Pa's mind, the people were saying, "Hey, that's the dad of the kid who killed Billy Lee Madden." It was heartbreaking for our family, and I can't even imagine how Billy's family was coping.

Eventually, Dad returned to Hereford. He and my mom got back together, and they married in December 1961, right in the middle of my mom's senior year of high school.

My mom and dad (above) married in December 1961, right in the middle of my mom's senior year of high school. I was born the next year.

Dad went to work for Turner Drilling awhile but ended up working for the City of Hereford like my grandfather. He worked on a truck picking up brush, limbs, and grass clippings while Mom finished high school.

Seven and a half months later, on August 4, 1962, along came me, Robbie Lynn Leffel, born premature. I weighed just four pounds, 13 ounces, and had to stay in the hospital a few weeks, but eventually I came home a healthy little boy. Everyone was nervous because I was premature, but super excited. I was the first child for Mom and Dad and the first grandchild for both sides of the family.

CHAPTER 3
The Good Life

As the first grandchild for both sets of grandparents, I was the luckiest kid on the planet. They were all crazy about me and spoiled me from that moment on. I got a lot of attention.

My mom's parents were farmers who lived just west of Hereford. My grandfather was James Clifton Price, but everyone called him J.C., and my grandmother was Janie Novell Price. What I remember most about Pa Price was his hands, rough and thick. Also, he could drive his truck really fast going backwards, which he did all the time checking the irrigation pipe as it pumped water down the rows to water the crops. It always amazed me. And man, my grandfather could talk. We'd go to town, and he'd see someone and they'd start talking, and it could go on for what seemed like hours, at least to a little kid.

My grandmother, Nanny Price, was so kind and one of the best cooks I've ever known. She cooked three meals a day, every one of them full meals—sausage, bacon, and eggs for breakfast, fried chicken and gravy for lunch, and another full meal at dinner. I loved her cooking.

I adored my grandparents so much, on both sides of the family, and loved spending time with each of them. It's crazy, but I can still remember their phone numbers, and it's been at least 25 years since I dialed them. I definitely count it a blessing to have had the privilege of knowing all four of my grandparents. Words can't explain the love and joy I experienced from those relationships.

Meanwhile, my parents were adjusting to life with a baby, which included work and a lot of baby diapers. I don't think it was much different for many people their age. My dad was smoking and drinking, but to be honest that seemed like the norm with all the people my parents hung around. Smoking was commonplace for just about everyone in those days. My mom eventually picked up the habit, as well.

As far as I can remember, life was good—at least from my viewpoint. Between my parents' friends and all their cousins living nearby, they socialized a lot, and drinking was usually involved, though nothing stands out to me as out of the ordinary. It was just their way of life.

As I got older, Mom got a job working as a secretary for an airline cropduster in Hereford, and I started going to a babysitter. Life was good. I was happy just being a kid and playing and living the good life. Plenty of fun memories come from those days, such as the day my dad brought an armadillo home from a trip to east Texas. He tied a rope to its tail so I could hold onto it. I remember being scared the armadillo would turn and chase me, but I held on tight, and it was one of my happiest days.

My childhood included plenty of happy memories, too, such as the time Dad brought an armadillo home from a trip to east Texas.

My dad raised greyhound dogs to hunt coyotes, and he had a pen full of them in our backyard. I used to play with them all the time. Once I remember making myself a sandwich and sitting out there with those dogs in their pen, enjoying my own picnic.

Another time, I busied myself picking up cigarette butts beside the house. I was maybe four or five years old at the time, and I remember getting my neighborhood friends and lighting up those butts for the kids next door to smoke. It was a blast until the neighbor lady caught me, and I ran as fast as I could and hid under my parents' bed.

Ah, the good times.

CHAPTER 4
Fresh Starts and Hidden Bottles

But trouble was brewing, even though I didn't know it at the time. When I was about five years old, I heard about a fire over at a city-owned building outside of town. I remember my dad talking about that fire, saying people thought he'd been the one to set the building ablaze. He denied it. I think he had to make a statement to the police, but that is about as far as it went. Still, there was bad blood between my dad and his boss, and they didn't like each other. Word spread. Conflict grew.

Our time as a family in Hereford was coming to an end.

Soon, my parents and I moved to Amarillo, Texas, which was the largest city in the Texas Panhandle. It felt like moving from the country to the big city. The good news is it was only an hour away from Hereford, so we could still see my grandparents from time to time. My dad got a job at Bell Helicopter working on and building actual helicopters, and Mom went to work for a lawyer as a secretary.

My family was excited to get a fresh, new start in the big city. This was by far the best job my dad had ever had, with good pay, good benefits, and at the time what looked like steady work for years to come. I was turning six in August of that year, which meant I could start school at Wolflin Elementary.

I was the youngest in my class, which might explain why it was my first time to attend first grade but not my last. That's right, I did so well the first time they suggested I try again. Back then, they did not have kindergarten, and I was very young for my class, so school was a real struggle, and honestly, I just wasn't mature enough. I remember enjoying school and making lots of friends, but my classwork was not good.

At that time, we lived across Interstate 40 from my school, and I remember one day, my mom was delayed so I decided to walk home. No one stopped me or questioned what I was doing—they didn't do that back then—so I just took off on my own. I had to cross the overpass to get back home. It's crazy to think I was at school alone, outside waiting, and no teachers were watching over the kids to make sure they got picked up. Life is so different today.

Needless to say, I survived the walk, though Mom about had a heart attack after she found out what I did.

My parents were working hard and actually doing pretty good. Amarillo felt like a positive change for our family.

A year later, we moved to the northeast side of Amarillo, closer to Dad's work. I started first grade again, this time at Forest Hills Elementary. But within six months we moved from one rental house to another nearby, and I had to change schools again. This time I ended up at Whittier Elementary.

School was much easier for me the second time around. Our family started to establish roots in the community, and my baby sister Lorrie Ann was born in 1969. It felt like things were going well. When I was in third grade, we were allowed to go home from elementary school for lunch, and of course no one was home at my house. So I started a little business—I decided to bring kids home for lunch and fix them sausage and eggs and take their lunch money, which back then was forty cents apiece. Business was good for a few days—until I got busted when my parents wondered where the food was going. They all got a good laugh out of it. I am so thankful for these happy times. We were a family of four now, with Mom and Dad working, and school and daycare and all the other challenges of life going on around us. We lived in this house another two years, and then we moved again just a few blocks away.

But my dad's drinking was becoming more and more prevalent.

While we were doing OK, getting by, I began to notice little clues about my dad's struggles with alcohol. I remember finding vodka bottles all around the house, hidden under couches, under cushions, and in various other places. Mom and I both knew his drinking was becoming a problem.

Once I found a bottle of vodka under the couch and showed my mom. We decided to pour it out, fill it up with vinegar, and put it back where we'd found it.

Years later I asked my dad if he remembered finding and drinking that.

He laughed and said yes. He said he'd already been drunk when he drank it and thought, "Man, this stuff has a weird taste!"

CHAPTER 5
Alcohol Takes Control

I remember Fridays when my dad wouldn't come home from work until really late. It was because he'd stopped off at the bar. All of us knew why he wasn't home, even my little sister Lorrie Ann, who was about two years old at the time. Mom would make the best of it, fixing dinner and turning on the TV to distract us from the truth—his drinking was becoming a problem. I know it was tough on my mom, but she held us together. This pattern continued for quite some time, and the tension grew thick in their relationship.

One night when I was about 10, I was in my room and I heard my mom screaming and crying. It sounded like it was coming from her bedroom. I crept down the hall to see what was going on.

I walked in to see my dad with a gun in his hand.

"I'm just gonna kill myself!" Dad threatened, his eyes wild.

I froze, terrified.

Mom grabbed the gun from his hands and disappeared to hide it.

I could tell Dad was drunk from the way he was slurring his words. I couldn't figure out what he was talking about—something about how my grandfather blamed him for something, but I don't know.

I was so upset and scared. Behind me, Mom came back into the room and said something quiet and soothing to him.

"Go on back to bed, Robbie," she told me.

But I couldn't move. What was going on? Why would he do something like this, threaten to kill himself? Would he hurt my mom?

Fear coursed through me.

Dad eventually calmed down, and finally we all went to bed. I'm not sure how much sleep we got, but we made it through another day.

But that night haunted me, not only his threats and how scared my mom seemed, but what my dad might have meant in his babbling about my grandfather.

I didn't find out about the accident until I was a teenager. I believe my dad mentioned something in passing about it, so I went and asked Nanny Leffel, and she told me a little, though it was years before I knew the full story. At the time of the incident between my mom and dad, though, it was clear my dad was tormented day and night with guilt. I could tell that much from the drinking and the rage that felt like an undercurrent in our home.

Looking back now, I wonder: Did my dad somehow blame my grandfather for the accident that took his friend's life? Maybe he did—maybe if my grandfather had not left a loaded gun in the closet, the accident would have never happened.

Even with all this going on, life had the semblance of normalcy. My mom had changed jobs and now worked at First National Bank of Amarillo, and she was doing well. One month, she was chosen as employee of the month, which was a big deal for her and for the family. The bank set up a time for a photographer to take our family picture at a park, and the picture was published in the local newspaper, the *Amarillo Globe*. We were all smiles in those pictures, but that was just how it looked on the surface. It certainly was not the reality at home.

Still, looking back, I am so proud of my mom. She was holding us together and thriving at work. She was like a celebrity, at least in my eyes. She was amazing.

There were some good times during these years. Dad and I both really liked to fish, and one day he bought an old fishing boat. It wasn't much, a 14-foot aluminum boat with a hand-operated motor on the back. Still, I was so excited, and so was he. We started making a few trips to Lake Meredith north of Amarillo to a place called Blue West to do a little fishing. We'd stop on the side of the road and pull out our flyswatters to catch some grasshoppers for fish bait. It was so much fun.

Before we got to the lake, we made our customary stop at the liquor store to buy beer or vodka. I hated those stops, but I told myself it was nothing. He'd drink from the time he bought it until it was gone. I was always concerned. After all, we had to drive home later. Thank God we always made it home safely.

One month, Mom was chosen as employee of the month, and a photographer took our family picture at the park for the local newspaper. We were all smiles in those pictures, but that was just how it looked on the surface. At home, reality was far different.

Another thing I really loved was to go watch big-time wrestling with my dad. We'd watch Dory and Terry Funk, Man Mountain Mike, Ricky Romero, and many others. Once I even got to meet Andre the Giant— what a huge man! On Saturdays one of the local television stations in Amarillo would have actual wrestling matches at its studios, and the one time we went to watch was the time Andre the Giant was there. He was truly a giant. His hands and feet were so massive that he didn't look real. He was a gentle giant, though, as he was so kind to all the kids at the studio that day.

I was so into it. My buddies and I would put all the big-time wrestling moves on each other, pretending we were real wrestlers ourselves. On Thursday nights, they had live wrestling matches at the Amarillo fairgrounds. My dad would take me, and after we'd been there for a while, he'd say he was going to the car. But he wouldn't return.

Later, after the matches were over, I'd make my way back to the car and find him there, passed out. I guess that was good—at least he could sleep it off a little before we had to drive home.

But it soon became all too clear: Dad had a problem. A big one. And I know it was impacting my parents' marriage.

It was also impacting him at work. One Friday, my dad didn't come home from work. Finally, about 9 p.m., someone began to pound on the door from the garage into the house. I was worried—no one should have been able to get into that door through the garage.

My mom opened the door.

And there was my dad, with blood all over him.

He'd been in a wreck and somehow gotten himself home. We were scared to death. Dad was cut up pretty bad, but overall he was OK. The blood made it look a lot worse than it was. He'd been lucky.

But we couldn't deny it anymore. The alcoholism was escalating and now impacting the entire family. Every day we were all on edge, not knowing what was next. Would he come home? Would he be drunk? If he didn't come home, where was he, and was he safe?

With all these questions circling through my own mind, I can only imagine what my poor mother was thinking.

CHAPTER 6
Good Time Charlie

Still, though we had a lot of tough times, I have some good memories. I loved to play sports, and initially basketball was my favorite. I remember begging my parents to put up a basketball goal in our front yard. Finally, with the help of Pa Price, they saved up and had a new basketball goal installed beside our driveway.

I was so excited, and so were my neighborhood buddies. We played basketball from sunup to sundown. We played so much the front yard was just dirt—we had no grass. My parents didn't care about the grass, thank goodness. I signed up and played for the local team, and I loved it.

My dad was not athletic at all and not interested in any sport except basketball. I'm not sure why he liked it. He couldn't really dribble or shoot the ball, and I'm not even sure if he knew the rules.

One year the basketball team I signed up for didn't have a coach. Guess who volunteered? Yep, my dad! We were awful. I'm not sure we won a single game. But I loved playing, and him being a part of it made it more special.

On our last game of the season, one kid on the team hadn't scored a basket all year. Finally, the kid caught the ball and threw what seemed like a half-court shot—and made it! All our jaws dropped.

Then we realized… he'd made the shot for the other team. He'd shot at the wrong basket! You can't make this stuff up. I remember we all laughed so hard, and my dad looked so happy.

Another thing I remember is the red El Camino Dad drove. I loved that car and even promised myself when I grew up, I was going to have a car just like dad's. I'm not sure why I liked it so much—maybe it's because we went hunting and fishing in it. I can still see him driving it, still see those vodka bottles tucked under the front seat.

Looking back, what's amazing to me is that even after the gun accident of his youth, my dad still taught me how to shoot a shotgun. One weekend, he took me out driving around in the country and brought his double-barrel 20-gauge shotgun. We were looking for rabbits or something to shoot at, and he asked me if I wanted to shoot his 20-gauge.

Of course I said yes.

"Now hold on tight, or it will pop up and hit you in the nose," I remember him saying.

Well, guess what? He was right. It hit me right in the nose.

For a moment, I couldn't breathe. I was stumbling around, crying.

"I can't breathe! I can't breathe!" I remember saying over and over.

I know he was chuckling to himself because I sure chuckle looking back on it.

My mom was a champ this whole time, doing her best and really doing it by herself. She worked, cooked, did laundry, cleaned house, took me to sporting practices, all while trying to protect us from what was going on between her and Dad. I don't know how she did it. With all the stress and pressure of day-to-day living, it had to be overwhelming working, trying to raise two kids, and taking care of an alcoholic husband. I am so thankful for her because I don't know what would have happened to us without her fighting to protect us from the ugliness of his struggle. Though I knew some of what was happening, I didn't see or hear all that was going on behind closed doors. She tried to give us as normal a life as she could under the circumstances.

I remember a song by Danny O'Keefe on the radio around that time called "Good Time Charlie Got the Blues." I heard it all the time, and boy, did the words hit home! It has stuck in my mind ever since.

My dad loved that song, and soon enough, it became his nickname: Good Time Charlie. I think he earned the title for sure. In fact, "Good Time Charlie" is actually on his gravestone. I think the nickname stuck because Dad certainly did like to have a good time, but there was also a sadness to the song that really went along with him and his daily struggles. One of the verses was, "Some gotta win, some gotta lose, good time Charlie's got the blues." His name, the lyrics to the song, and the way his life played out all made the nickname very fitting.

Thankfully, my dad was not a violent drunk, at least not to me, and I don't think with anyone else. I remember when he was hanging out and drinking, he'd sometimes grab money out of his pocket and give it to me. Most of the time I'd just see him drinking beer at the table or in the living room. Usually he would slip off to sip his booze in secret, stashing it in hiding places around the house where he'd take a few shots of vodka or whatever was the drink of the day. Then he'd come back, pick up his beer, and start back where he left off.

But finally, his drinking got so bad he went to rehab for several weeks. I remember it well. I was 12 years old, and I knew something had to change. He was drunk all the time, missing work, not coming home—just a total disaster. I'm sure my mom threatened that if he didn't get help, she was going to leave him.

I must admit the few weeks he was gone, it was nice. We didn't have all the drama around Dad and his drinking.

He came back sober, and I was so happy. He wasn't slurring his speech or stumbling. He could carry on a conversation, and you could see him, not the alcohol. It was great, such a change for the better.

Unfortunately, it was short-lived.

About six weeks later, I came home from basketball practice one evening and saw him working on his boat.

Then I saw the six-pack of beer sitting by the boat. My heart dropped, as if it were broken. No. Not again. I'll never forget that feeling for as long as I live—for I knew what was coming next. In his mind I'm sure he was thinking, "I'm fine. What's a few beers?"

But the beer was the key, and the door opened to a downward spiral.

CHAPTER 7
Jesus Saves

My family was not consistent with going to church, but when we did go, Dad was never with us. When I went to Nanny and Pa Leffel's in Hereford, we always went to church with them. Nanny and Pa never missed, attending twice on Sundays and every Wednesday evening. At times, both would lead the music.

I can still remember my grandpa sitting in his chair reading his Bible. He was quite a character—in church on Sunday and cussing like a sailor on Monday. Honestly, many of us fall into to that category at times.

Nanny, also known as Aunt Tater to many in the family, was the rock for everyone. I saw her as a four-foot, ten-inch giant, quiet, soft-spoken, and worried about everything and everybody until the day she passed. She loved Jesus, and once she told me she gave her life to Jesus when she was just five years old. She said a traveling preacher came by their house out in the country when she lived in east Texas, and the preacher couldn't read, so his wife would read the scripture and he would preach. Nanny sat in a tree, listening intently, and that's the day she asked Jesus into her heart.

I love that story—even at five years old, she knew something was missing in her life. I'm not sure about my grandfather, but I do know he was very dedicated to attending church and was there basically any time the doors were open.

I was 12 years old the day I gave my life to Jesus. My grandparents' church in Hereford was having a weeklong revival, which was basically a daily church service focused on sharing the good news of Jesus Christ. On Sunday evening, the last event of the revival, my grandparents and I were sitting in the back row of the church. Honestly, I don't think I was really paying attention at all.

That's when the pastor started talking about our need for a savior.

"We are all sinners," he said, "and we are separated from God. But God made a way for us with the birth of his son, Jesus Christ. Jesus came to live his life and die on the cross to pay for my sins. He died and was resurrected three days later."

This message moved me in a way that was so unexpected. No one had talked to me about my faith, no one was pressuring me, but I felt the overwhelming need then and there.

The Lord called me that day, and I was overcome with the understanding that Jesus was talking directly to me.

I remember crying my eyes out as I walked down to the front of the church to pray with the preacher. I remember being so happy to accept Jesus as my Lord and savior. I am so thankful my grandparents were so faithful in attending church, as it was their faithfulness that brought me to Jesus.

After, I was so excited about my new relationship with Jesus that I couldn't wait to be baptized. The little church in Hereford was very small and didn't have a baptistry, so we had to find another place.

A month or two later, a baptism was set up for a Sunday after church at a local motel swimming pool. I remember the day well. My mom and both sets of grandparents were there, and I hoped but didn't know if my dad would show.

At the very last minute, Dad showed up. I was so excited! This might have been the only religious event my dad had ever attended other than a few funerals.

After the baptism, my dad came up and hugged me, but don't remember him saying anything special. Everyone was happy, and we all went down the road to a local restaurant for lunch—all except Dad. It was such a special day to me: Not only did I tell the world I love Jesus, but also my dad cared enough to show up.

CHAPTER 8
Downhill Spiral

About the time, my parent's marriage began to go downhill fast. Even after his second stint in rehab, Dad's drinking was causing more and more problems. Mom kept insisting he get help.

I knew their relationship was in trouble, and I was afraid what would happen to the family if this continued. One terrifying day, my dad drove me and my sister to Hereford to stay with my grandparents. I don't know what was going on—if he was taking drugs or something, or if he was drunk—but I remember being scared to death on the ride from Amarillo to Hereford. There on the highway from Canyon to Hereford, he started dozing off, swerving all over the road. I was sure we were going to wreck.

I shook him, waking him up, and he was OK a few minutes, then he fell asleep again. My little sister Lorrie was with us, but I'm not sure she really knew what was going on. She just kept saying, "Wake up! Wake up!"

God was looking over us for sure. I have never experienced a longer 30-mile ride in my life.

We made it to my grandparents' safely, but then I worried about him driving back to Amarillo. It all worked out, but it's a feeling I'll never forget. I loved my dad, but I hated what was happening to him. I don't think any child should experience that kind of fear ever.

Dad continued to spiral downward. He lost his job at Bell Helicopter and got a job working on grain elevators, which had him on the road traveling a lot. It was an awful situation for him. Their group of men would work during the day, then hit the local bars at night. This only magnified his drinking problem.

All I wanted was for him to be sober. What I have learned is no matter how much you love an alcoholic, your love won't make them quit. If it did, this whole situation would have been behind us.

I know the entire family wanted him to recover. I remember being with Nanny Leffel, and we were talking about alcohol.

"Robbie, promise me you won't drink when you grow up," I remember her saying.

I hugged her. "Don't worry. I will never go down the same path as my dad."

Little did I know that was a promise I wouldn't keep.

Late one Friday night, there was a knock on the door. It was the police—and my dad. He had a broken nose and was covered in blood. Thankfully, he wasn't in trouble with the law. They'd just brought him home.

Dad said he got off work, cashed his check, and went to the bar. He said someone must have known he had cash in his pocket, because when he was leaving the bar to get into his car, someone jumped him, hit him with something, and broke his nose. His cash was gone.

My mom was skeptical of the story. Even worse, now his entire paycheck was gone, and bills were still coming in.

The inevitable result of all of this loomed: Divorce was not far off.

All this time, I couldn't understand why he drank. It was destroying our family. As a young kid, I didn't understand the internal turmoil he was going through from his past. The grief was destroying him—and our entire family.

Soon my parents separated. My dad was a terrible mess, and my mom was doing her best to be the rock for the family, but I knew she was wearing down.

One day, Mom came home from work, and she was just a wreck. My dad was gone, probably drunk, it was dinner time, the bills were coming in, and she had two kids to take care of with no help, all while trying to hold down a job. I'm sure the situation was overwhelming her.

She rushed out of the house, crying.

I followed her.

"I have to get out of here," she said, climbing into the car.

Then she backed out of the driveway and drove away.

I stood there, at a loss for words. My head was spinning. Is she coming back? What am I going to do? What about my sister? I will never forget that feeling of panic.

Thank God, my mom came back in about 20 minutes. She just needed to clear her head.

All of us were in pain. My mom was doing all she could, and I am sure it was overwhelming. I don't know how she kept it together.

CHAPTER 9
Shock Treatments and Near Misses

One morning in school I heard my name in the middle of my seventh-grade class. An office aide motioned, and I followed her down the hallway to the front office. Some people from my mom's bank were there. I didn't know any of them.

"We're taking you to your mom, Robbie," was all they told me.

We got in the car, and they drove me all the way to Hereford, to my mom's parents.

That's when I learned the awful news—my grandmother, Nanny Price, had passed away of a heart attack. She was just 55.

I was devastated. My grandfather, Pa Price, was a total wreck. All he could do was cry, and this upset me, so all I could do was cry, too. The entire family was in shock. Her death was completely unexpected. My grandmother was so very special to me. She loved me, and she always told me that. My mom, her sister, and her brother got to work planning the funeral. It was a very sad day.

The following day, my dad came to see my mom. He was very kind. He loved my grandma, and I know he was sad for my mom. That's really the last time I remember them being together without some friction or fear.

A few days later we had the funeral. My dad attended, and I saw him at the burial. I don't think I've ever cried so much in my entire life. This was my first experience losing someone close, and it hurt. I remember my mom and her siblings were sitting in the row in front of me. I was crying so hard and couldn't stop. My grandfather reached back and grabbed my hand to comfort me. I will never forget that gesture as long as I live.

After that, Mom tried to get our family back on track—as normal as we could be under the circumstances. It wasn't long before she met a man at the bank. She wasn't divorced yet, but it was only a formality of some paperwork, because my parents were never going to reconcile. They started dating, and this man, Dewayne, eventually became my stepfather.

As you can imagine, I was not happy about this new man in her life. And meanwhile, my dad was drinking himself to death. My sister and I would see him every week or so, and I always suspected he was drinking. I was miserable thinking about the future. What's going to happen to us? Mom is with this man we barely know—is she going to marry him? Would we have to move away from my friends? My whole world was falling apart, and I had nowhere to turn.

One day, I was out playing with friends, and Dewayne was at our house, working on the fence in the backyard.

That's when my dad showed up—with a gun.

They told me later Dad was really out of it, on drugs or alcohol and clearly had the intention of shooting Dewayne, and Mom was frantic. Lorrie was there, and I am not sure what all she saw, but I'm sure it was not good. She was only six years old. Somehow my mom got my dad to leave without anything terrible happening.

I came home to find my mom crying her eyes out like a crazy woman, and I had no idea what had happened. Thank God no one got hurt. I was so scared and confused, but deep down I was thankful I hadn't been there to witness it. I'm not sure I could have handled it.

My dad was staying at a friend's house at the time, and shortly after this, he started having seizures. I believe the seizures were brought on by the alcohol or drugs he was taking. Finally, they took him to the hospital and then to a rehab facility. His life was spinning out of control.

I just felt torn. I was mad at my dad for tearing apart our family, and I was afraid he was going to drink himself to death. My parents were going to divorce, my Nanny Price had died, a new man was dating my mom, and life as we'd known it was over. I knew Mom was doing the best she could, and to this day I know in my heart that if she'd not gotten us away from my father, he would have destroyed our entire family. But as a kid, your family separating is your worst nightmare.

My dad spent a couple weeks at the rehab facility, and by now the divorce was in process. When he got out, he seemed to be better. He started coming around to see me and my sister, but you could tell he was still not right. He was distant, like he was caught up in his own head.

Later he told me they'd given him shock treatments in rehab. That's where the doctors attach leads to your body, then send electrical shock waves through your body. He said the treatments were intense and knock you out, and then you're asleep for several hours. The idea is to make you forget why you are so upset. I have no idea if it worked on him, but maybe it helped the pain go away for a while.

One day, Dad came by, picked us kids up, and we went somewhere. All I remember was the ride home. That memory is seared in my brain.

We were at a stop sign, right across the street from our house, and I remember him glance directly at a car coming toward us.

Dad drove right out in front of that car—like he was aiming for it.

I saw the whole thing, and it was not an accident. I know God was protecting us because somehow that other car did not hit us.

It's crazy—you could see our house from that stop sign. What was he doing? Why would he pull out in front of that car? We could have been hurt or killed. Why would he put us in that danger?

These answers I will never know, but his troubles ran deep.

I remember my mom asked for $150 per month as child support for both kids. Wow, a hundred and fifty bucks—not much! I think Dad paid that once, and that was it.

She could have had him put in jail, but she never pursued it. I'm sure she knew the truth: He couldn't take care of himself, much less us.

CHAPTER 10
Football and Jesus

In the spring, my mom married Dewayne and we moved from Amarillo to Durango, Colorado, for about six months, and then moved to Canyon, Texas. During our time in Durango, we didn't have much contact with my father. My grandparents—his parents—stayed in touch, and I think they sent some money to Mom to help us. Nanny Leffel loved my mom so much, and she knew Mom had done the only thing she could to protect us.

We moved to Durango to get away from my dad, I'm guessing. My stepdad had several jobs in the brief time we were there, but they just weren't enough. Our stay in Durango was short-lived, but it was such a beautiful place. In that brief time, I had the chance to make new friends and got to explore the mountain right behind our house. But like all Texans, I couldn't wait to get back to Texas. We finished out my seventh-grade school year, then moved to Canyon, just outside of Amarillo.

Finally, I was back in Texas, and much closer to my grandparents. It was the beginning of my eighth-grade year, and I started playing football and absolutely loved it. Our team wasn't great, but I loved the people, and they welcomed me with open arms. I will be forever grateful for those friendships and the kindness of the many families I met in Canyon.

Home life was still tough, especially now with a new stepdad, who I was not crazy about. His kids were brought into the picture, too—what a mess! It felt like a circus at times. All of us had issues we were dealing with, and that only added to the drama. But even though I didn't get along with Dewayne, I have to give him credit. He provided a roof over our heads and food for us to eat when my own father didn't. I am forever grateful to him for providing for all of us.

I really lost track of my dad during this time. I know he was drinking himself to death because Nanny Leffel would keep my mom posted. Mom needed money, but he was no help at all. He'd work a little, make some money, buy a bunch of booze, and rent a motel room or find an abandoned house for several days. Then he'd just drink until he passed out, wake up, and start all over again.

When I was much older, Dad told me he'd go sit at the gravesite of the young man he'd killed in the accident. This made me consider the pain and guilt he was living with every day—maybe every hour. I can't imagine what it must be like to wake up with that guilt every day.

The only way he knew how to deal with that guilt was alcohol.

Liquid self-destruction.

I threw myself into sports, but I also made good grades. My mom would come watch my games and practices when she could, but I don't think my dad ever came to any of my sporting events, though at the time it didn't really bother me. I played football and basketball and ran track. Anything they offered, I wanted to play.

By ninth grade, I was active in the Fellowship of Christian Athletes. I was lucky enough to attend an FCA conference in Dallas with a coach and a friend, and it was amazing! Two of the speakers were Tom Landry and Roger Staubach of the Dallas Cowboys. I loved the Cowboys, so that was a treat, and the conference reignited my passion for Jesus.

All three of us came back with a new fire for Christ. We started sharing Jesus with all our friends, reading our Bibles together, and praying for each other. The numbers grew in our meetings, and I know many gave their lives to Jesus during this time. It was a very special season for me, and I will never forget it. My walk with the Lord was growing.

Everything was looking good, and I started my sophomore year at Canyon High School.

Then, a few months into school year, I got the news: Our family was moving.

Again.

My stepfather had gotten a job as a foreman on a ranch in Pampa, Texas—about 75 miles away.

I was so frustrated with the move. I'd finally gotten established, made some great friends, and was doing well in school, then here we go. Time to move again.

But life doesn't always go your way. That was a truth I'd already learned.

Meanwhile, my dad was continuing to spiral downward with his drinking.

By now I had my driver's license. Before our official move to Pampa, I decided to drive to Hereford with a friend of mine, Dennis Hill. To this day, Dennis is one of my dearest friends and ended up being best man in my wedding.

When we got to Hereford, we stopped in to see Nanny and Pa Leffel.

"Your dad's at Alan Brook's house," Nanny told me. Alan had been a drinking buddy of my dad's for years. They seemed to always find each other, and trouble was just around the next corner.

Of course, Dennis and I decided to go by and say hello.

When we walked in, Alan immediately jumped behind the couch. I think he was high.

My dad was sitting in a chair staring at the TV.

"Hey, Dad, what's up?"

He looked at me with a blank stare, and I could tell he had no idea who I was.

Man, that hurt—that my dad could look right at me and have no idea his son was standing right in front of him. He was either drunk or high, I don't know which.

Finally, I said, "Dad, it's your son. Robbie."

Then slowly, he acted like he knew me.

Dennis and I got out of there as fast as we could.

CHAPTER 11
Drinking Bars and Prison Bars

I was lucky I liked sports, because it was a great way to make friends. It didn't take long for me to settle into my new life in Pampa. There, I met one of my best friends, Tom Clay Coffee. Everyone called him Clay. Clay was a tough cowboy kid who drove a Grand Prix. He was a great friend and still is to this day.

Pampa was a small town in the Texas Panhandle, and its major industries were oil, gas, ranching, and some manufacturing. We were living on a ranch just north of town, by the airport, and my stepdad was now foreman of a ranch, so I got introduced to ranch life—basically, horses, cattle, and working your tail off.

And as in many small towns, what did the kids do for fun? Drink beer. Well, forget that promise I'd made to my grandmother. I jumped right in and started drinking with my friends.

The first time I drank a few beers, I got sick and threw up in Billy Ward's parents' front yard. That should have been my clue that my body didn't care for alcohol, but that was just my start.

Small town, football, driving around the drag for hours, chasing girls, and fighting—what a life! As you can imagine, my walk with the Lord began to take a back seat. While I was still participating in FCA and was even voted president of the club, in my heart I knew I was not living a life worthy of that role.

So what did I do? Instead of manning up and changing my ways, I resigned and kept doing all the things I wanted to do. My friends were great, and I love them to this day, but the path I was heading down was not God-honoring, and I knew it.

Yet that didn't stop me.

My high school life was good. Popular, I played sports and served as student body president my senior year. I would have never run if it hadn't been for Heidi Jean Allen, who talked me into running with her. Heidi was very pretty and super popular. Everyone loved Heidi, and I know I wouldn't have had a chance without her. I must have been the lamest leader a school could have, as I was not into school politics. I was into having fun and partying with all my friends.

While I was living large, my dad continued to get into trouble. I would drive to Hereford every few months and see Nanny and Pa Leffel. Once, Dad was there, and we had the only harsh words I ever remember having with him.

We were talking about my sister, Lorrie. I had a summertime job and worked some side jobs, so I had a little spending money, but my sister was too young.

"I can take care of myself, but you need to step up and do something to help Lorrie, Dad," I told him. I'm not sure where I got the nerve.

It was a waste of breath and time. All he could do was worry about his next drink. I was so frustrated with him.

At one point during my high school years, Dad ended up in jail in Hereford, though I'm not sure for what—probably something alcohol-related. I remember going to visit him in the Hereford Jail.

That was a weird experience—going into the jail cells and sitting at a table with my dad, just talking. It was actually a good conversation, oddly. Dad was sober and seemed glad to see me. We had a good chat, I got up to leave, and the guards slammed the cell door behind me.

"Not every kid gets to have this kind of experience," I remember thinking.

Home life was tense. My stepfather and I did not see eye to eye, and we had some rough times. He was verbally abusive, and a few times it got physical. The worst for me was the mind games he'd play, threatening me if I told my mom anything. I'm thankful my mom was there to stand up for me. If not, it could have gotten really bad.

At one point I left home because I felt his abuse was too much. My mother was devastated. I was only gone for a few days. My high school football coach, Larry Gilbert, opened his home to me, and I slept on their family couch. I will never forget that act of kindness. I love that man and am thankful to say Coach Gilbert and I are still good friends. More importantly, we are brothers in Christ.

My mom begged me to come back, and I did only because she told me she loved him. I was ready to pack our stuff and get out.

When I got home, my stepdad kept his distance. I'm sure Mom must have read him the riot act.

The next few years passed quickly. Even though my stepdad and I didn't get along, he and my mom made sure to attend my important events.

I finished up high school and got ready to take off to college.

All my high school buddies were going to Texas Tech, and my grades and SAT scores were enough to get in the door.

While I thought I was ready for college, all I was ready for was a party. And that's exactly what we did. My friends and I hit the bars every chance we could, and this showed in my grades. By midterm, my grades were two Cs and two Ds.

That was a wake-up call. I buckled down and finished up the semester with all Bs. I was finally figuring out what it was going to take to get through college.

Still, I continued to drink and party with the best of them. And as far as a spiritual life, I had none. I turned my back on God and stopped attending church.

I didn't know it at the time, but my story was that of the prodigal son. I knew the Father, but I chose to follow the ways of the world. I wish I could say it was a quick return, but it would be a long journey back to him.

†

Meanwhile, as I took baby steps toward getting my life together, my dad was going in the opposite direction. His drinking was bad, and he was running around with people who had the same problems he did. They fed off each other.

One day, they needed money for booze and decided to rob a place to get money. My dad was the getaway driver.

They got caught, he went on trial, and was found guilty.

He was going to do some time in prison.

I remember not being all that upset about it. "Maybe that's the best place for him," I thought. He can't get booze if he's in prison.

CHAPTER 12
Surprise!

My dad did about a year in prison, then was sent to a halfway house in Lubbock, the city where I attended college.

I went to see him a few times. Dad was living in an old motel—a dump, to say the least. It was hard to believe this was where the state sent the formerly incarcerated to reintroduce them to civilian life. The place felt dark, and you could tell trouble was around every corner.

But Dad seemed content there. He was happy to be out of prison. He told me how tough prison was. Since he was older, the other inmates didn't really bother him, but for the young inmates it was bad. He told me you learn quickly who is in charge.

He said it only took him one day to learn that, when you were spoken to by the prison guards, your answer better be "Yessir, boss." Dad just wanted to do his time in the halfway house and get back to Hereford.

I had started dating the girl who would eventually become my wife, Darenda Wise. Darenda was from Brownfield, Texas, a small town outside Lubbock. One afternoon, I took her with me to meet my dad, and incredibly they hit it off. My dad really liked her, and they got along great. I think I might have run for the hills if my boyfriend had taken me to meet his dad at a rundown halfway house, but she stuck around. He was doing good and staying sober—at least for a while.

Beyond that, ten other guys and I had started our own fraternity. I won't say it was life-changing, but I did make some lifelong friends who I love to this day. It also brought me to Darenda, for she and I met at a party neither one of us should have been at. I know I should have been studying, but we hit it off.

Before you knew it, I had proposed, and she'd said yes. We were young, and I was so full of myself chasing the world and all it had to offer. This created problems between us, and we broke up a time or two. We continued to see each other on and off, but I was completely focused on myself. Still, I knew I was lucky to have someone like Darenda, a great girl, interested in me.

In early August, just before the beginning of our final semester of college, we found out Darenda was pregnant.

All my thoughts were selfish: My life as I know it is over. What am I going to do?

I knew in my heart the right thing to do was get married. We had a child coming.

I'll never forget going to her parent's house in Brownfield to tell them the news. We were both concerned about how they would respond.

We sat down at the kitchen table, and I was so nervous my knees were shaking. I shared the news, and it was quiet for a few seconds, but it seemed like an hour before they responded.

They were shocked and I'm sure disappointed in the circumstances, but they were very supportive of us and our decision to get married.

We wasted no time. Three weeks later, Darenda and I married at First Baptist Church of Brownfield. Most of the family, including Mom, Dewayne, and Lorrie, came to the wedding. The only ones missing were my dad and Nanny and Pa Leffel. My grandparents wanted to come, but my grandmother was sick and she was the driver. I have no idea why Dad didn't come.

Suddenly, my head was spinning. I'm married! I had one semester of school left and a baby on the way. I also had absolutely no walk with the Lord. Selfish, full of myself, and immature, I had turned my back on God.

And I certainly was not prepared to be a dad or a husband.

†

Meanwhile, my dad had left the halfway house and returned to Hereford. All his good intentions didn't last long—soon he was back to his old ways, running with his drinking buddies, and staying drunk.

My poor grandmother witnessed it all. She did everything she could to help, but nothing seemed to work. She lived every day in fear my grandfather would have a seizure or my dad would get drunk and hurt himself or someone else. Not to mention, my grandfather and dad were always at odds and had their own battles, one with epilepsy and the other with alcoholism.

It must have been hell living in that house.

CHAPTER 13
The Real World

Darenda and I soon got a crash course in what it was like to be married and live with each other. It wasn't easy—we were in our last semester of school, and all my college buddies were still around. I wanted to be hanging out with them, not tied down with the responsibility of a wife and a baby on the way.

This created some tension for sure. But Darenda was right—I needed to be moving away from that life. I fought it all the way, but she stood her ground.

We made it through our last semester, and in December 1984, we both graduated from Texas Tech—Darenda five months pregnant.

Our graduation was a big deal for our families, as we were both the first to graduate college. Pa Leffel was so excited he planned to ride a Greyhound bus from Hereford to Lubbock so he could attend my graduation, as Nanny Leffel was not able to come. When Pa Price heard about the bus, he went and picked up Pa Leffel and drove them both to Lubbock for my graduation.

I can still see them beaming with pride at my graduation—my two grandfathers. I knew my life was not going as they would have hoped, especially with Darenda and I having to get married the way we did, but getting that degree was a huge accomplishment in their eyes. I had the greatest grandparents ever.

I'd gotten a Bachelor of Business degree in petroleum land management, a field in high demand when I'd started college. But by the time I got out, the oil industry was in a bust, not a boom. I had a tough time landing a job, and the placement center at my college had no program for my degree, as it was very new one.

One day I went to the college placement center and wrote to every oil company whose name and address I could find, sending each one of them a resume. Weeks went by with no response.

Then I got a letter from Standard Oil of Indiana (Amoco) requesting I come for a job interview in Tulsa, Oklahoma. I didn't know a soul in the company, but I jumped on a plane and flew to Tulsa. I met some representatives from the company who took me to their offices. I had a three-hour interview, and then I went home. That's it. I had no clue how the interview went.

The following week, I got a job offer. Praise the Lord! One interview, one job offer: to be an associate division order analyst. The offer was for $19,500 per year. Darenda and I were so excited. We thought we had it made.

After Christmas, we loaded up the U-Haul, pulling my wife's 1970 Buick Wildcat and headed to Tulsa. We didn't know anyone, and we didn't have a place to live, but we had a job.

Looking back, I know God saved our marriage by moving us away from Lubbock. Had we stayed, I would have continued partying, and my wife would have run home to her parents.

But now we were 500 miles away from Lubbock with only each other to depend on. It was not easy, and I was not a good husband. I was selfish and only wanted what I wanted. My wife was pregnant and living far from home with a jerk. I know this had to be hard on her. But she was so excited to be a mom.

Then, on April 4, 1985, our first daughter, Danielle Nicole, was born.

Having a child changed everything for both of us, but it really hit home with me. I was now responsible for a wife and a child. Danielle was perfect, and I was in love from day one.

However, while I thought we'd made it with that big salary, I was wrong. After bills, a car payment, student loans, taxes, insurance, and diapers, we were broke. That $565 bucks every two weeks didn't go very far.

My father-in-law, who didn't have much money, sent us $50 to help, and all I could think of was how I had to get him paid back as soon as possible. My wife's oldest brother, Donald Craig, also helped us get by. He was always so helpful and giving to us. I will never forget his generosity or his love for my wife and our kids.

We were scraping by.

Meanwhile, the baby was growing, and Darenda said we needed to start going to church.

But I wasn't interested.

"Fine," my wife said, so she found a church and started attending on her own with Danielle.

I felt a little guilty but still didn't go. Her Bible study was called WWACA: Women Who Attend Church Alone. Now how does that make a guy feel? A little embarrassed!

So I told her I would go to church, but that was it.

"The weekend is my only time off, and I deserve a break," I told her. Man, was I full of myself. Football came on at 11:30 a.m., and that was my priority.

During all this, my dad was still on his path of destruction. On occasion, I'd call my grandmother, and she would let me know he was still drinking. Most of the time, he was living with my grandparents, which was terrible for everyone. He and my grandfather constantly argued, and my poor grandmother was in the middle trying to play peacemaker—a losing battle.

I didn't talk to my dad much during this time in life. To be honest, I was not all that concerned about him. I had my own family to worry about and care for.

Darenda and I wanted to have another child, so we started trying. By God's goodness, on November 18, 1988, our second daughter, Deidra Danay, was born. Another perfect, beautiful child. These two little girls had stolen my heart, and I was crazy about them both.

Work was, well, work. I wasn't crazy about my job, but it paid the bills. I would occasionally drink but wouldn't say it was creating problems at home. We really wanted to move back to Texas, like any good Texan would want, but God clearly wanted us to stay in Tulsa for now.

I finally got the opportunity with Amoco to transfer to Midland, Texas, working in the crude supply group. We were so excited to move back to West Texas, where we'd be much closer to our families.

Still, we were thankful for our time in Tulsa. We'd lived there four and a half years, and we both grew to be better parents because of the experience.

CHAPTER 14
On the Move Chasing a Career

We drove into Midland, Texas, in May 1989 and rented an apartment. We were thrilled to be back in Texas and closer to family, and I was excited about my new job. I couldn't wait to get started.

I went to work for a man named Steve Setliff, a great man who loved Jesus and lived it in the workplace. Steve consistently asked us to join him and his wife, Teri, at church. Darenda and I finally accepted and started going.

I knew deep down I needed to seek Jesus, but my selfishness continued to keep me away. I was there but I wasn't, if you know what I mean. Darenda's faith was growing, however, and she was focused on making sure our girls were in church even if it was without me.

Steve left a lasting impression on me. He walked the walk at work and everywhere else. Another thing that stood out to me was that Steve did not drink. That was odd, especially considering the business we were in. The crude oil purchasing and marketing business was very customer-focused, so you were with customers all the time, and 90 percent of the time alcohol was involved.

Not for Steve. He'd graciously decline and move on. I didn't know it at the time, but that had a big impact on me. I didn't drink much, and I think it was because of Steve's influence. But Steve wasn't around all the time, and when he wasn't, I would definitely turn it up a notch or two.

Midland was great as we got to be relatively close to family for a couple of years. It was only about 200 miles from Hereford, and once my grandparents and my dad drove down to see us. It was a great visit. Dad was sober for a change, and he spent time with the kids. They called him "Pa

Pa Charlie."

My dad was in his mid-forties at the time, but he looked much older. All the smoking and drinking were taking their toll. He'd already had his lower teeth pulled and wore dentures. As he sat on the back porch holding Danay, my youngest daughter, he gave her a big shock by taking his teeth out.

Danay was amazed. "Pa Pa Charlie took his teeth out!" she began screaming to anyone who'd listen.

We all got a good laugh. Looking around that day at my family gathered together, I was thankful for some happy memories. Even if they were few and far between, they were good for the soul.

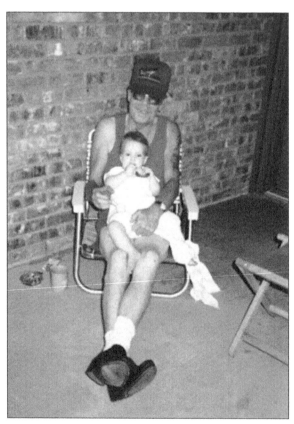

Dad, here holding my daughter, Danay, was only in his forties when this photo was taken, but he looked much older. The smoking and drinking had taken a toll, and he'd already had his lower teeth pulled and wore dentures.

My mom was living near Lubbock, and we would see her and my stepdad occasionally. They stayed in touch and came down a few times to help us with some house repairs. We had a good relationship with them. It was nice being close to family.

Then it happened. We'd been in Midland a couple of years when what I'd been dreading finally came to pass: my transfer to Chicago, Illinois. Amoco headquarters.

My new boss, Pat McGannon, walked into my office with the news. "Mike Foley is about to give you a call about a job in Chicago."

I knew it was coming, but we didn't want to go. I even tried to get a job with another company in Midland.

But it was just not meant to be. The paycheck was moving, so we were moving.

What a culture shock—going from Midland to Chicago! My daily routine included driving to the train station at 5 a.m., then taking a 40-minute train ride to Chicago. I had a mile and a quarter walk from the train station to the Amoco offices, and I was in my office chair around 7 a.m. At 4:30, I reversed the trip and was home around 6 p.m.

So this is what moving up in the world looks like. We were broke, with no extra money at all. My boss, Mike, would buy me donuts and cinnamon rolls every once and a while, and that was like Christmas. He really tried to look out for me and make me feel welcome.

But I was trying to get back down south before the moving truck ever arrived.

We found a house in Aurora, Illinois (home of Wayne's World). Our house price doubled from Midland, yet we'd lost 700 square feet of living space. What's not to like, right?

As soon as we got moved in, Darenda looked at me.

"We need to find a church home," she said.

She jumped on it. Within a month, Darenda had found a little Baptist church not too far from our home. Again, she was being the spiritual leader of our home. And again, I was still reluctantly attending.

It was so important to her that our kids be involved in church. It should have been important to me, but I was too absorbed with work—and myself.

We only lived in Illinois a little over a year. It was a short stay, but we made some good friends: Jim and Carol Novak and Tim and Melanie Russell, who we still stay in contact with. Also, my old boss, Steve Setliff, had moved to Chicago, and he kept tabs on me and checked on us. He was a great man. He and Teri had a going-away party for us when we moved. What was so amazing about it is they found out who our friends were and invited them to their home and they didn't even know them.

I talked to Mom occasionally, as she was better about staying in touch. But I didn't have much contact with my dad during this time. I'd talk to my grandparents, and they would give me updates.

Nothing much had changed with him. He'd be sober a while, then drunk a while.

†

We moved to Houston in 1992 and lived there only nine months before we got transferred again, this time to Denver, Colorado. Even though our stay was short, the first thing Darenda did was start looking for a church. The pattern continued—she led our family, and I reluctantly followed.

The good news about the move to Denver was I finally achieved my dream job: being negotiations representative for Amoco Oil. All my hard work was starting to pay off. We moved to Highlands Ranch and got started on the new job. I was focused on work, Darenda was taking care of the kids, and of course she found us a church.

I actually started going to church a lot more, but I was a fake. On Sunday morning I was helping the little ladies in the door, then Monday it was back to the ways of the world. In this job, you were always with customers, and drinking and socializing was very common. My problem was I didn't want to have just one. If we were going to have one, we might as well make it a party.

I believed the lie that I had to do this as part of my job, and that's what I told my wife. The problem was I was drinking too much, and when she'd question me about it, I'd just lie. I never got in trouble with the drinking except the most important place, which was home.

We loved living there. Our neighborhood was great, with kids and families outside all the time. Our all-time favorite neighbor was Bev Suttman. She was so down-to-earth and adored my wife and kids. I got to work with some amazing people: John Moore, Pat McGrath, and Ray Banks, to name a few. Those guys were so smart I don't know how I ever managed to get to a place where I was working side-by-side with them. They were great to me, and I still cherish their friendships.

Then we got the phone call: My dad needed open heart surgery. He was just 53. It was unexpected, so I was scared.

My whole family drove to Amarillo to see him.

Dad was on a ventilator. It was an awful sight—his whole body shook every time the ventilator forced him to breathe. When I walked in and saw him, I thought there was no way he'd live through this. Pa Leffel stood crying over my dad as he just lay there. After all those years of fighting, yelling, and screaming at each other like they hated each other, now I could see through it. Pa really loved my dad. He just didn't know how to show it.

Amazingly, Dad pulled through surgery and made a full recovery. Doctors told him he needed to stop drinking and smoking or he'd be dead within a couple of years. I think Dad took that as a challenge. He chose to prove the doctors wrong by not quitting.

†

A year later, Pa Leffel had a stroke, and my grandmother just could not take care of him any longer. She had no choice but to move him to a nursing home.

I remember I came from Colorado to Hereford to talk to Pa and tell him what we were going to do. He didn't say much, but I know he was heartbroken.

When we came to town, we'd all go see him, but he really couldn't communicate. He could barely hold his head up, and it seemed like he cried the whole time we were there. It was devastating to watch him like this.

About four months after he went into the nursing home, he passed away. It was the only day my grandmother hadn't gone to the home to see him. She'd gone that day to Lubbock to see some family.

She never forgave herself for not being with him on his last day.

I don't even remember my dad during this time. I'm not sure what he was up to, but my guess is it involved drinking.

We buried my grandfather a few days later. Quite a few family members came to town for the funeral. It was bittersweet, saying goodbye to my grandfather and catching up with relatives we had not seen in years.

Dad showed up and behaved himself. He stepped right in and welcomed everyone, and it seemed he enjoyed visiting with all the family.

When we were wrapping things up and people started heading home, I sat down with my dad.

"I'll take care of Nanny," he promised.

I had my doubts, but I didn't feel like we had any other options at that time.

CHAPTER 15
The Reload Revival

In November 1996, we got transferred back to Houston. I was more excited than the rest of the family. They loved the Colorado mountains, the neighbors, and their friends, but I always knew I wanted to move back to Texas. Not only do I love to hunt and fish, but many of my close friends also lived in Texas.

We got moved in, got the kids in school, tried to get our routine in place—the usual. When we'd been in town about a month, Darenda said it was time. We needed to find a church. This was no different than all the other places we lived. We began our search, looking around and attending area churches to see if we could find a church home, a place that felt like we belonged. I reluctantly tagged along.

After six months, we finally ended up at Bear Creek Baptist Church on Clay Road. The church was fine—I really didn't pay that much attention—but I knew my wife was happy, so that was good with me. Then it was back to the norm: church Sunday, and chasing the world and its ways the rest of the week.

Chasing the world meant drinking—and lately, I'd been drinking a lot. My job had me interacting with customers all the time, and normally we would have a few drinks. Many times I had too much, or I'd call my wife and lie about where I was or how much I'd had to drink. I knew she wouldn't be happy, and who wants to ruin a good party? I am so thankful I never got in trouble with the law, but that could have happened very easily, which would have jeopardized my job as well as my family. Drinking and driving is so dangerous, not only for you but for others. Thank God nothing ever happened.

We built a good life in Houston. Work was going well, and the kids were as busy as ever. Darenda started going to church with the kids on Wednesday nights to an event called Reload. Clint Paschall was the student minister, and Darenda was blown away by what she was hearing and seeing those nights.

"Come on, Robbie. Come with us!" she'd plead week after week

I continued to fight it. I could tell God was speaking to her, and she was getting excited. But nope—I wasn't going.

One weekday afternoon, one of the guys from work was leaving for a new job so we decided to celebrate with him. We went to a small bar in west Houston and started drinking and playing pool. These few drinks turned into a drunken stupor for me. Though I made it home by 6 p.m., I was so drunk I staggered in the house went straight to our bedroom.

It wasn't much later that I got sick and threw up. I took a shower, cleaned up, and went to bed.

The next morning, you could feel the tension in the air.

I've never seen Darenda so furious.

"I will never cover for you with your kids again," she told me.

I couldn't blame her. This hurt, and I knew she wasn't joking. While it didn't stop me from drinking, it definitely got my attention.

It's crazy. I'd watched my dad struggle with alcohol, watched the damage it caused our family. Now here I was, heading down a similar road.

Darenda continued to take the kids to Wednesday night church. The service focused on junior high and high school kids. She begged and begged me to go.

Finally one evening I did. And surprisingly, I felt like God was talking directly to me.

I remember we were in the church gym, and it was absolutely packed with kids. They had a small group of kids who played worship music before Clint, the pastor, would speak.

Clint's message was so powerful and convicting, and it hit home with me. I went again the next week, and the week after that, and the Lord started working on my heart, opening up my eyes to the sin I'd been living in for so long.

Soon I became deeply ashamed. I knew the Father, yet I'd turned my back on him for almost 20 years. I was overcome with guilt and shame.

But God welcomed me back with open arms. I truly repented of the sin in my life.

That's when God really started to speak to me through His word, our church, and other Christians he was putting in my path. God was moving, and my life began to change.

Instead of worrying about myself, I started looking for ways to help others. God was doing a big work in me.

I now know He was preparing me to be a witness to my father and share the loving grace and forgiveness of Jesus Christ. But at the time, all I could sense was something big, something important and meaningful, stirring inside me.

God was now my first priority, then my family.

I was still working in a commercial job, out entertaining customers and drinking occasionally. One week, I remember taking a group of customers fishing to Lake Texoma, about four hours away. We went out to dinner, then to a local bar. I remember drinking quite a bit, but nothing really stands out to me. We closed the place down and headed back to our motel.

But the next morning, October 1, 1998, was the day everything changed.

I remember waking up and walking outside the cabins. I could see the lake beyond. As I walked, I began thinking about the night before and what I'd had to drink. I didn't feel terrible, but I didn't feel good.

Then I felt like I heard God telling me: Enough with the drinking. Who are you following?

I know God called me to stop, and I have not had a drink since that day.

What I didn't know was how God was going to use this later.

To be honest, I wasn't sure how others would respond to my sobriety. Would it impact my work and ability to work with customers? Would my friends treat me any differently? Would I be accepted?

All these thoughts were going through my head, but God had spoken to my heart, and I knew regardless of any personal costs it was time. God knew what was best for me.

That's when my life really started to change.

The Lord began to speak to me through the youth ministry at our church. I had turned away from the Father, who loved me, to chase the world for the last 20 years. My heart was breaking and my sorrow for my sin was overwhelming to me.

I felt like the prodigal son welcomed home with a celebration that was not deserved. My heart was changing, and God was changing me.

I noticed my compassion toward others was changing, too. Before, if I saw someone hurting, I would walk right by, never giving a second look.

But now my heart ached for those suffering, and I'd seek them out. My views as a father and husband shifted, as well. I started putting their needs before my own.

It exploded from there—my language, my view of money, my heart for the lost. Church was no longer a dreaded chore but a joy, a place to learn, to grow closer to fellow believers, to serve others, and to celebrate the joy of my salvation.

I know I was saved when I was 12 years old, but my relationship with Jesus did not really begin to grow until I was 36 years old.

CHAPTER 16
Jesus Prepares Me

Before I knew it, my wife and I were teaching in the youth at our church. Me, teaching? Really, could God use a person like me who is flawed, broken, and selfish?

The answer is yes. He has a plan for each of us.

We started bringing as many kids from our neighborhood to church as we could. We even traded cars to get a Chevy Suburban so we could fit more kids in the car to take to church. Now, I won't say we didn't have too many people in the car at one time, but I can say we wanted these kids to hear about Jesus, and our youth pastor had a true gift of sharing the gospel of Jesus with them.

My relationships began changing, and my co-workers could see something was different. It was all because of Jesus—He was now in control, not me.

I began sharing my faith with others and genuinely making an effort to live out my faith at home, work, and wherever else God took me. My faith was growing, and I regularly spent time in God's word and in prayer.

Who is this guy? I wondered one day as I looked in the mirror. God was changing me from the inside out.

A friend of mine from work and church, John Caldwell, reached out to me a few months later and asked if I would be his accountability partner. Accountability basically involves two people of faith holding each other accountable to our Christian values. We met maybe three times, but then John got transferred to another city. I was disappointed and wanted another Christian man to help me in my walk with Jesus.

Karl Kurz's name came to mind. Karl was a friend I had made through business and had known about 10 years. Karl was different, special. He'd been walking with the Lord his whole life, not anything like me.

Karl agreed to be accountability partners, but he was not 100 percent convinced this was a great idea. Honestly, it took almost a year before both of us fully trusted each other enough to share our true struggles. The topic of accountability is a book in itself, but I will say this relationship changed my life for the better and helped me in my walk with Christ.

I remember Karl told me once that I was vindictive. I promised if he ever said that again I'd get even. We've had many a good laugh about that comment, but the truth is, it hit very close to home. Karl has gone on to be the single biggest male influence in my life. I love and cherish his friendship. What's even more impressive is I know I am only one of many men who would say Karl is one of the biggest male influences in their life.

As for my dad, I wasn't keeping up with him. I might talk to him a few minutes if he answered the phone when I called Nanny Leffel, but the conversations didn't amount to much. He was still on the roller coaster ride of alcoholism, and I didn't want to have much to do with him.

I remember that year, a couple days after Christmas 1998, my wife, kids, and I were in Brownfield, Texas, at my wife's parents' home. We had a wonderful time together with her family, and everyone was happy and doing well.

The phone rang, and it was Nanny Leffel.

"Honey, I'm worried about your dad. I can't get in touch with him, and I haven't seen him in days," she said. I could hear the concern in her voice. "I'm afraid he's in some … some cheap motel or abandoned house drinking himself to death. Or worse, already dead."

I got in the car and drove the 100 miles to Hereford. I was worried and beyond frustrated—my dad had promised to look out for her, but he had broken so many promises in the past. This was nothing new. Now here my grandma was, having to look out for him.

Nanny and I checked the old motels and abandoned houses he'd been in before. We checked the hospitals. Basically, we checked every place we could think of except one: jail.

Finally, I called the police station and asked if Charles Edwin Leffel was one of their prisoners.

"Yes, he is," the lady at the police station said.

"Hallelujah!" I couldn't help but reply.

She was shocked by my response, but I told her we were just thankful to know where he was and that he was alive.

I hugged my grandma, kissed her forehead, and drove back to Brownfield. Now maybe my sweet grandmother could at least rest knowing he was safe and alive.

I see now that God was stirring my heart. While I wasn't thinking about my dad much beyond the Christmas fiasco, when I did, I felt a deep sadness, both for him and for my grandmother.

He was destroying his body, and it was like torture to my poor grandmother. I couldn't understand it at the time, but God was preparing me for a few very intense days with my father that would change both of us forever.

CHAPTER 17
The Call for Help

In late February 1999, my phone rang.

"Robbie, this is Anne Crouch," came a sweet, kind voice over the phone line. "Your grandmothers in the hospital, and your dad's been drinking on and off for two weeks."

As you can imagine, I was upset. A quick call to my Nanny Leffel reassured me that while she was indeed in the hospital, she was resting fine, and it was nothing serious.

Then I called my dad.

His words were so slurred I could barely understand him, but I did understand one thing.

"I'm going to drink until I die," he said.

I gripped the phone, beyond angry. "When you get ready for help, you can call me."

Then I hung up.

Over the next two days, I tried calling my dad. Sometimes he would talk, but sometimes he'd just get mad, cuss me out, and hang up the phone.

I had no hope for him. I just knew if he didn't change his ways, he would die drunk.

That broke my heart.

That Friday evening, I was heading home from playing golf with my friend, Clay Coe. We'd had a great day, maybe not the best scores, but some great fellowship.

As I drove home, I tried to call my dad.

He answered, called me a few curse words, and hung up.

I had no idea why he was so mad. I just blamed it on the booze. The words still hurt, but I knew the booze was doing a lot of the talking.

I got home around 6, and my phone rang—and it was my dad.

"I need help," Dad muttered. "I can't do this on my own."

Then he hung up.

Shock became surprise. But my first thought was that if he was asking for help, then I need to help.

My wife and two daughters were not at home, and I couldn't reach them. I quickly checked for flights, and the last one out of Houston was that evening at 8:30. I had a free Southwest Airlines ticket, so I called and they got me booked. By 7, I'd left a note on the table for my family and was on my way to the airport.

It was midnight by the time I arrived at my grandma's house. Nanny was still in the hospital.

I was scared about what I'd find inside. I didn't know what to expect, not to mention how Dad would react.

"Lord, please give me strength and courage to face anything I might see," I prayed.

I went in and found he was asleep. The house was a wreck, with multiple bottles of Mad Dog 20/20 and cinnamon schnapps all over the house.

As he slept, I tiptoed through the house, throwing away all the booze. I also found some pornographic tapes, which I destroyed and threw away as well. You could just feel the darkness all around the house, and all around him. I was emotionally disgusted with what I was seeing, but I was glad my dad was still alive.

Now came the moment of truth: I woke him up.

Dad was startled, but at least he remembered calling me.

"You need to take care of my mom," was the first thing he said to me. "She's in the hospital."

"I'll go see her in the morning, Dad. I promise." I'd already talked to her and knew she was OK.

Dad peered around. "Where's my booze? I need a drink so I can come off easy."

How could that be the right thing to do? But Dad was adamant.

"If you don't believe me, call my buddy John Bill," Dad said, starting to get worked up. "He'll tell you."

So I called John Bill. By that time, it was one in the morning.

"No way," John Bill told me. "That's the worst thing you can do."

So I stood my ground.

Dad's face turned red, and he balled his fists. "Why, you no good—"

Furious with me, Dad began to cuss me with every breath he had.

I tried my best to tune him out, instead focusing on the house and on him. He looked awful. He'd knocked over the furniture and thrown up all over the bed, on his pillows, and on his clothes.

I did my best to clean him and the room up. He was still cussing me with every breath.

He was so angry with me. "You don't understand you can't come off booze cold-turkey. You're a worthless piece of sh—" he'd say. "You don't care about me. If you did, you'd give me a drink, you sorry son of a —."

It felt like I was in a fight with the devil for his soul. The venom coming from him was terrible. All he wanted was a drink, and he didn't care who he hurt to get it.

After a couple of hours, he finally settled down and went to sleep. I went over, laid by him, held onto him, and prayed the Lord would soften his heart and rid him of this demon of alcohol in his body—and take away that filthy language. He hardly said another cuss word over the next two days. The Lord is awesome.

Watching someone come off the booze is awful, and as dad told me later, it gets harder and more intense each time you try. I was really worried he wouldn't live through it. I prayed for strength for both of us. After all, he'd had open heart surgery just three and a half years earlier, and doctors had told us then if he didn't quit smoking or drinking, he wouldn't last another two years.

I knew this might not end well. It only worried me more and more.

As Dad started coming off the booze, he began throwing up at least every 10 to 15 minutes. He'd lay down for a minute or two, get up, smoke a cigarette, take a drink of water, and throw up.

This cycle happened over and over. That first night, I stayed up with him all night and was exhausted. I can't imagine how he felt. I'm sure he didn't sleep more than 10 minutes at a time that whole period. It continued for several days.

The whole time, I just kept praying: Please, God, help us. Give us strength.

CHAPTER 18
The Struggle for True Forgiveness

The next morning, Saturday, Dad woke up and was a little more coherent. He could talk and make some sense. But he still wanted another drink.

We talked about a lot of things over those dark days. As you can imagine, there was not really much reason to hide anything at this point. Dad was a wreck.

I began telling him he needed to turn his life over to Jesus because there was no way he could beat this on his own.

"I know," he said. "I've been trying all my life, and I always fall back to the booze."

That broke my heart.

I looked at him. "Dad, have you ever accepted Jesus as your savior?"

He waved a hand. "Yeah, when I was a little kid. But the only reason I did it was because Red told me to." He'd always called his father Red—not Dad, not even Father. Their tension ran deep.

At one point, he told me about a lady he was really crazy about and how she'd run off with another man. He said it made him furious, so he decided he'd just get drunk. Here we were, several weeks later, and he was still drunk.

I shook my head. "Dad, that's one reason you cannot put your faith in another person. At some point they'll fail you—we'll all fail you—no matter who they are. But Jesus? He's rock solid. He is never changing, and He will never forsake you."

I read him some Bible verses—I can't remember what they were—and we both started praying for the Lord to help.

By the end of that day, my dad asked if I would lead him in the prayer to ask Jesus into his heart.

"Dear Lord Jesus…" I began the prayer.

But then my dad said, "Stop! I can't do it."

I frowned. "Why, Dad?"

Dad put his head in his hands. "How can God forgive me when I can't forgive myself?"

I knew he was talking about Billy Lee Madden, the boy from the gun accident.

I didn't know what to say. I thought about it for a little while as we both sat in silence.

Then I started telling him the story of the apostle Paul from the Bible, and how Paul had persecuted Christians and had Christians killed. Yet God used him to share the gospel of Jesus with the Gentiles, and really the whole world.

We continued to talk, and the following day my dad said he was ready to ask Jesus into his heart.

So I prayed with him. When we finished, I told him from that second forward he didn't have to worry another minute. He was forgiven, and he would be going to heaven.

I was overcome with joy. After all these years, my dad—with all his struggles and all his pain from the death of that young man—was giving everything over to Jesus. The only true way he could receive peace and forgiveness. What a huge blessing.

Throughout all this, we were still dealing with the alcohol withdrawal. It was awful, as he was throwing up nonstop. Then he'd try to smoke and sleep, but nothing seemed to calm him. He continually asked the Lord for help.

At one point, Tag Johnson, his Alcoholics Anonymous sponsor, called to check on him. Tag told me to make him the "Tag special," some warm tea and honey, and maybe he could hold that down. Dad's buddy John Bill came by the house a little while so I could go check on Nanny and get some groceries.

When I got back, we tried the Tag special, and it worked. Finally, Dad had something stay down.

We had a lot of time to talk over those days. Dad shared about all the guilt he felt. He said he experienced deep hurt daily over the afternoon he accidentally shot and killed Billy Lee.

Later the same day, Dad was sleeping. That's when I heard a yell.

"Robbie!" Dad hollered. "I can see Billy's face and the blood running out of his body!"

That was the guilt that had been haunting him for 42 years.

"Dad, the Lord knows it was an accident," I told him. "The Lord has forgiven you."

We also talked about Red, my grandfather. My grandpa must have been pretty abusive. In fact, my dad said he beat him until he was 16. That's the day he told my grandfather if he ever did it again, he'd kill him.

Dad resented my grandfather, always telling me how much he hated him. But that day, before we quit talking, he said something I'll never forget.

"I really loved that old man, Robbie. I shouldn't have been so mean to him."

The Lord was definitely softening his heart. It was another rough day, but it seemed we were starting to make some progress.

On Monday, my grandma was going to be released from the hospital, and I planned to head back home to Houston. Two of my grandma's close friends—Anne Crouch, who'd called me that day, and Rosalie Willis—were there, helping to take care of her. Both of these ladies my grandmother had met through a support group for people whose family members had some type of addiction, and they'd been so wonderful to my family.

When my grandma got home, I could tell she was scared.

But my dad hugged her and told her he was sorry—and that he loved her. Then he told them all he had accepted Jesus as his Lord and savior.

Anne Crouch was so excited she hugged his neck.

I headed back to the airport, hoping and praying the worst was behind us.

CHAPTER 19
Obstacles

That Saturday, March 6, was my dad's 57th birthday. I never would have dreamed he'd have lived this long based on what he'd put his body through for all those years. I called and wished him a happy birthday. We had a good talk.

But no one knows the temptation or the struggle an alcoholic faces every day. The next Wednesday, March 10, I decided I'd call my dad and Nanny before church.

He was drunk. My fears were realized.

But he was still alive.

I asked to speak to my grandma, but she was gone. I found out she'd left him, gone to stay with her friend, Peggy James.

When I finally talked to Nanny, she said some people in Hereford were going to get Dad some help. My dad apparently got violently angry with her because she refused to give him money for booze. When he doubled up his fist at her, that's when she decided to go stay with Peggy.

Dad just said he didn't want their help.

I began trying to call my dad. I dialed him over and over. If he answered, he'd cuss me out or just hang up.

By Friday, I'd decided I needed to seek some professional help for him. Even though some people from Hereford had tried, I learned until he asked for help, there was nothing that could legally be done.

Thinking I could change that, I made a few phone calls. I called Justice of the Peace Johnny Turrentine, who referred me to Jim Doss out of Amarillo. What a sweet man he was. Jim was so kind to me and tried every way in the world to help me, but he also gave me the cold hard facts: If my dad chose, by law he could sit there and drink himself to death.

He gave me some phone numbers, and I wound up talking to Basin Detox out of Stanton, Texas. Over the next five or six days, I spoke with several kind women who worked there—Maria, Rita, and Lisa. They all tried to help me, asking so many questions: Does he have Medicaid/Medicare? What is he drinking? When was his last drink? Has he been using in the last 72 hours? Has he ever seen a psychiatrist? Has he had hepatitis? Has he had heart problems? Is he allergic to anything?

All these questions had to be answered, but there was one more, and only he could answer that one: Why do you think you need detox?

If Dad didn't think he needed the help, the facility was not going to waste time and resources.

I got everything answered except the last question, and Dad was approved for a detox program in Iraan, Texas.

Then I called him.

"Dad, do you want help?"

He said yes.

I said, "OK, then answer this question. Why do you think you need detox?"

Apparently, that crossed the line. Dad cussed me out and hung up.

I kept calling back, but he'd just pick up the phone and hang up or not answer at all.

I was so upset, but I asked for the Lord's strength and wisdom. After all, if Dad wouldn't ask for help, we had limited options.

Then I waited.

†

A couple more days went by, and I couldn't get in touch with my dad. I called Deaf Smith County Judge Tom Simon and his assistant, Diana, who referred me to Gene Reynolds, an alcohol counselor who also happened to know my dad. He told me to call the Crisis Stabilization Center in Amarillo. I was so relieved—finally, a real lead on some help.

But when I called, I got an answering machine. This was just unbelievable to me. I finally got a call back and learned, to my dismay, the program had been discontinued a few weeks earlier.

I called Gene back.

"Gene, what do I need to do to have the judge commit my dad?"

There seemed to be no other options.

Gene told me to call Northwest Texas Hospital and talk to them. I called the main number and got forwarded to the emergency room—then no one would answer. I felt like I was being tested.

So I persisted. I called back and finally got in touch with a woman named Elise, who explained what to do. While the hospital did not treat chemical dependency, she told me, they did treat depression. She gave me some ideas on how to fill out the forms the county judge would need to consider committing him.

Diana, the judge's assistant, was wonderful—but yet again we hit a stumbling block. It was as if everything in the world was determined to stop my dad from getting the help he needed. Diane tried to fax me the forms, but the lines at my office weren't working.

Then my cell phone rang. It was my wife.

"Peggy James called and said your dad's on his knees asking the Lord to take his life," Darenda told me breathlessly.

Darenda recounted how Peggy tore into him and told him to get up and straighten up. Then he reportedly told Peggy the magic words: He wanted some help.

Maybe this would happen, after all.

I picked up the phone called him.

"Dad, do you want help?" I asked. "Why do you want to go to detox?"

Dad finally gave me an answer. He said he needed help—and he wanted it.

†

I tried to cover all my bases. I made my plane reservations, then called Diana and asked her to fax the forms to my house, and she did. If Dad backed out, I wanted everything lined up so the judge could commit him involuntarily.

When I got to the airport, I filled out the forms and tried to use a pay fax. Of course, it wouldn't work. The obstacles would have been laughable had they not been so dire.

I was frantic then. My 1 p.m. flight had been cancelled, but luckily there was another at 2. I wandered as I waited, looking for any office I could find, and found the Department of Aviation.

When I told the ladies my dilemma, they let me use their fax. Thank you, Jesus, for making a way.

I called Diana, she got the fax, and I got on the airplane. When I landed, I called Basin Detox. They had a bed for my dad in Iraan, Texas, if my dad would agree to go.

If not, we had one final option: The judge could commit him.

CHAPTER 20
The Ride

I got to Hereford at 5:30 p.m. and called Basin Detox to see if they had anything closer than Iraan, which was 300 miles south.

"Maybe Stanton, Texas," they said. Stanton was 100 miles closer, and on the way. I asked them to call my cell phone if anything opened up.

Inside the house, I picked up all the empty bottles and took them to the trash. My grandma packed a suitcase.

I woke Dad up. He had a bottle beside his bed, and I had to fight to take it away from him. He cussed me out for 15 minutes.

I got everything in the car laid out with a blanket across the backseat and a bucket on the floorboard—I knew he was going to be sick.

The adventure began.

Dad's last drink was sometime around 4 or 5 p.m., and we drove off around 5:45. He didn't waste any time. Before we could even get out of town, he was trying to jump out of the car. Man, this was going to be a long drive. I asked the Lord for protection and strength.

For the next hundred miles, Dad kept trying to jump out of the car, and I kept grabbing him and screaming. I called Basin Detox again and begged for them to let us go to Stanton because it was closer.

"He's drunk, throwing up, and trying to jump out of the car. If this is just a paperwork issue, get it figured out!" I hollered at Lisa, the lady on the other end of the line. "It can't be worth losing a life." This was crazy.

A short time later, a supervisor from Basin Detox called. In the middle of our call, Dad tried to jump out of the car yet again. I was screaming at him and the supervisor heard it all, but he just apologized over and over—there was nothing open in Stanton.

We kept on heading to Iraan. I was wearing out, and I still had 200 miles to go.

I called Darenda.

"Can you call Dan and Barbara?" I asked her.

Dan and Barbara Garlington were our good friends in Midland, en route, and I hoped Dan would agree to help me when I got to their town.

Dan immediately agreed. "Whatever you need, I'm here for you," he said when I called.

We made a plan that I'd call when I got close to Midland.

By now things were settling down and Dad was no longer trying to jump from the car, but he'd started getting really sick—and throwing up.

I kept giving him water as I drove, and he kept grabbing onto me, holding my arm and kissing my hand and telling me how much he loved me and that I was the best son a man could ever have. It was very sweet.

Then he started complaining about his heart hurting.

At one point, he clutched his chest and, all at once, fell back in the seat. For a few minutes, I thought the Lord may have just called him home.

"Lord, if this be your will, I accept it," I said and just kept driving.

About 15 minutes later, he started wobbling back up and talking. I was so relieved he was alive.

Then he passed out again.

I was in the middle of nowhere, and there was nothing I could really do for him, so I just continued to pray. I was scared, but also I was calm. I knew the Lord was watching over us.

I finally got close to Midland and called Dan. He met me at a gas station and drove the rest of the way. It was nice to have some help.

Before we got to Midland, my dad said he didn't want us to talk at all. But when Dan got in the car, Dad started asking him questions. Dad looked awful, and the smell in the car was terrible.

But Dan was a true friend. He just said, "Tell me what you want me to do."

Dad asked Dan if he was a Christian. Then he began asking questions about Dan's family. Dan was very kind and patiently answered all the questions my dad had for him.

Then Dad got quiet. I don't know if he was thinking or if he just passed out

We finally made it to Iraan about 11:30 p.m. and got Dad checked into this tiny little hospital in the middle of nowhere. He was freezing, but we got him checked in and got him plenty of covers to warm him up.

"Goodbye, Dad. I love you," I told him.

He said the same.

As I was leaving, I could hear him getting sick, and the noise echoed through the halls.

I knew the next few days were going to be rough. They were going to keep him five to seven days, then look for a treatment program. I told him before I left at least 10 times I really needed him to stay and not run off.

The last thing he said was, "I promise."

The rest was in the Lord's hands. Dan and I started back home.

It had been a long, crazy journey, and it wasn't over, but Jesus and so many others held my hand all the while and kept us safe.

I took comfort in knowing that even though he was fighting the alcohol, my dad had given his life to Christ, and that's really all I wanted. The thought of him dying drunk, alone, and separated from God was more than my heart could take.

CHAPTER 21
A Changed Heart

I wish I could say Dad never drank again. He had at least one more relapse after that, but God was with him and working on his heart. Based on an old journal I found after he passed away, his last drink was in January 2000. That was more than four years before his death.

What a blessing. I really never believed my dad would die sober, but thanks to Jesus and his newfound peace, he really changed over the last four years of his life.

After he got sober, Dad made sure my grandmother was taken care of. He made sure she went to all her doctor appointments, bought groceries, and basically did whatever she needed.

Dad tried hard to be a good son in his sobriety.

Dad was quite the character, really a funny guy. I would call every week or so to check in on them, and he always answered with a joke: "Sheriff's Office." "County Jail." "Police Station."

He fell in love with a cat he named Gladys, and four turtles he named Otis, Luther, Gomer, and Carolyn. I have no idea where he came up with the names. They were like his kids, and he took good care of them.

Our regular phone calls were often silly.

"Hi, Dad, what's going on?" I'd ask.

"Oh, Otis ran off with a stripper turtle and we haven't seen him in a week," he'd sigh, or "Gladys just mooned Granny."

I'd say, "Dad, you doing OK?"

And he'd reply, "Yes, and are you sleeping in the house yet?"

We almost always had a good laugh.

As I said earlier, my dad was crazy about my mom, and even all these years later he would ask about her, then he would ask, "How's my husband-in-law doing?" referring to my stepdad. That always cracked me up.

I would end by saying, "Stay out of trouble."

He'd reply, "That's good advice. You might try it yourself! Give the girls a smooch and I love y'all."

He always had something funny to say. The talk was all lighthearted and good for the soul.

Over those last four years, he turned into a hoarder and was collecting a lot of junk. Once I counted 13 lawn mowers in the backyard, an abandoned RV he'd found somewhere, and miscellaneous junk just everywhere. He also started cutting off two thirds of the brims of all of his hats. I guess he thought that looked cool. As long as he was sober, I thought they looked pretty cool, too.

Even though some of the things he was doing were strange, I didn't care. He knew Jesus, he was sober, and he was taking care of my grandmother. Such a change from the man who used to cuss me with every breath.

I knew it was because he'd found the forgiveness that can only come from putting your faith in Jesus. He'd tried finding that forgiveness in the bottle, in a marriage, and in his kids. But nothing could fill that hole but Jesus. God had taken a broken man, forgave him, and loved him. All our lives changed for the better the day he accepted Jesus. Dad still had a few battles with the bottle over the last half of 1999, but God had him and was not letting go.

Dad was getting some money from disability, and though it wasn't much,

In his last years, Dad got very involved with the local AA chapter in Hereford.

he started sending a little to my sister to help her. Lorrie had finished college and moved to Houston with her three boys, but money was tight, and she needed help. I was so thankful to hear he was trying. Even though he knew he'd failed her in the past, he was making an effort. I know it wasn't much, but it was long overdue.

In those last years, Dad got very involved with the local AA chapter in Hereford. He was so dependable they actually gave him keys to open and close the place—what a change! Dad made sure the coffee pot was on and all the ashtrays were out. He had his own chair up against the wall, where he always sat during the meetings. He loved the people there, and they loved him. He could relate, and I know his experiences helped others.

AA is anonymous, but when my dad died, several of his friends from the AA club invited me to a meeting. They wanted me to meet his friends and see where he sat.

It was great meeting them, but I must admit I couldn't wait to step outside and get a breath of fresh air. The minute the meeting started every person in the room fired up a cigarette except me, and it was nonstop until the meeting was over. But I didn't really care about the smoke—they were so real and genuine. They truly cared for each other.

He had a rough life, but in the end, my dad made a difference.

I remember the day my dad passed away. I was at work in Houston, and my grandmother called me. She told me he'd passed away in his sleep.

I was in shock for a few minutes. Then I thanked God for my father—and for God's forgiveness. I had the peace that surpasses understanding (Philippians 4:7).

While I was sad to lose him, I was thankful I knew he was with Jesus. I had spent most of my life worrying he would die drunk, alone, and separated from God. None of those worries had come true.

At his funeral I shared Dad's story from the accident through his salvation. One lady called me after the funeral.

"You have no idea the impact his testimony had on me," she told me.

I don't know if she gave her life to Christ or if He was speaking to her. All I know is my dad's life was not in vain. He made a difference.

✝

After the funeral, I started going through all his belongings. I found an old journal.

The next-to-last page was dated February 8, 2004.

"Thank you, Jesus," he'd written. "I have been sober 4 years 4 days. Took some scrap metal and sold it today." Then he penciled in February 9, 2004.

That's what he wrote just before he went to sleep. We don't know if he died on the evening of the 8th or early the morning of the 9th.

But for him, the next day never came.

This makes me think of all the people who think they can address their relationship with God tomorrow. We have no promises for tomorrow. We never know when today might be our last.

At Dad's funeral, one of his cousins, Chester West, told me I should put "Good Time Charlie" on Dad's gravestone. I wasn't sure about it, as I thought it might be disrespectful.

But when I asked my grandma what she thought, she was fine with it, so I told them to add it.

Rest in peace, Good Time Charlie.

CHAPTER 22
Forgiveness

The whole reason for this book was to give people a glimpse into the life of a person who was consumed with guilt to the point of trying to destroy himself. Guilt is a powerful tool the devil uses to keep us away from God. But God was there the entire time, waiting to give Dad forgiveness and grace through Jesus Christ. I'm glad my dad finally realized that.

We are not promised an easy road, but we are promised God will not forsake His children. I can't imagine the pain and suffering my dad went through from that accident that claimed the life of young Billy Lee Madden—and almost claimed my dad's soul had he not found Jesus in the end. I can't imagine the toll alcohol and cigarettes took on his body over all those years, but none of that compares to the glory he experienced the day God called him home.

My prayer is this story will encourage those walking in a storm alone, whether with a family member or a friend. Peace can only be found in Jesus Christ whether you are watching the storm or you're in the storm. Those storms can last a lifetime if you try to walk alone.

As I have been working on this book, the Lord has opened my eyes and heart to the importance of our relationships with our earthly fathers. I have spoken to numerous people about their relationships, and I am sad to say most of the people I spoke with had a struggle with their father or have a hurt they cannot release or forgive.

I didn't know it, but I was experiencing something similar—not with my father, but with my stepfather.

It was almost surreal for me to realize I was fine with my dad after all we went through with our family and his alcoholism. Yet I hadn't made that peace with my stepfather.

Dewayne passed away more than ten years ago, and he and I talked about our past once. He said he was sorry for the things he did that were wrong.

At the time I told him, "Don't worry about it."

But I didn't mean it. I didn't want to forgive him. I wanted to hold it over him, and I wanted him to pay.

Yet Dewayne wasn't even alive anymore. Who was I really hurting?

I had no idea the impact this was having on me and others all these years later.

Finally, I met with a Christian counselor and was advised to write down all the things I needed to forgive concerning Dewayne. I did, and it was a good process, but I still had more to do.

One day I started praying and looking at all the ways I had been wronged, and it was like God opened up my eyes. I saw that in some shape or form, these things I couldn't forgive were no different than the sins I had committed against God.

How did God respond when I asked for forgiveness? I was forgiven, no questions asked, with those sins never to be remembered again. Like the Bible says, as far as the east is from the west, so far does He remove our transgressions from us (Psalm 103:12).

The Bible is clear on the importance of giving forgiveness. In Matthew 6:14-15 it says, "For if you forgive others their trespasses, your heavenly Father will also forgive you, but if you do not forgive others their trespasses, neither will your Father forgive your trespasses" (ESV).

This is serious and not only impacts your earthly relationships but also your relationship with your heavenly Father.

I urge you to please make the effort to be at peace with everyone, even if you must swallow your pride to reconcile those broken or wounded relationships. I can say without a doubt outside of my relationship with Jesus, the relationships with my family and friends are truly my most treasured gifts.

I am incredibly thankful for this journey God has given me and all the people who have been involved along the way. I am forever grateful for all these people. To each of you, I love you and cherish your friendship.

My prayer is something in this book spoke to you and pointed you to Jesus—the only place we can truly find hope and true forgiveness.

Thanks, Dad (a.k.a., Good Time Charlie) for inspiring me to write this book. I love you, and I hope others facing the battles and hardships you faced will find the peace you sought for more than 40 years of your life.

Jesus was the answer.

Peace can only be found in Jesus Christ whether you are watching the storm or you're in the storm. Those storms can last a lifetime if you try to walk alone.

ABOUT THE AUTHOR
Robbie Leffel

Robbie Leffel, 59, has been married to his wife, Darenda, for 37 years, raised two beautiful daughters, and has three grandchildren. Leffel was raised in the Texas Panhandle and finished high school in Pampa, Texas, in 1981. He graduated from Texas Tech University in 1984. He worked in the oil and gas industry for more than 35 years until retirement in 2020. In retirement, he loves to bass fish and spend time with kids and grandkids.

Leffel loves Jesus, serves in his local church, is involved with a couple of men's Bible studies, and is always happy to share his testimony of how Jesus changed his life.

Made in the USA
Coppell, TX
08 March 2022

74681672R00057